The Inside Guide

MOVEMENTS FOR EQUALITY

# The Story of the Chicano Movement

By Amy Holt

Cavendish Square

Published in 2024 by Cavendish Square Publishing, LLC
2544 Clinton Street Buffalo, NY 14224



Website: cavendishsq.com



Library of Congress Cataloging-in-Publication Data

Names: Holt, Amy, author.
Title: The story of the Chicano movement / Amy Holt.
Description: Buffalo, NY : Cavendish Square Publishing, [2024] | Series: The inside guide : movements for equality | Includes bibliographical references and index.
Identifiers: LCCN 2023007107 | ISBN 9781502668202 (library binding) | ISBN 9781502668196 (paperback) | ISBN 9781502668219 (ebook)
Subjects: LCSH: Chicano movement–History–Juvenile literature. | Mexican Americans–Civil rights–History–Juvenile literature. | Mexican Americans–Social conditions–Juvenile literature. | United States–Race relations–History–Juvenile literature.
Classification: LCC E184.M5 H64 2024 | DDC 973/.046872–dc23/eng/20230221
LC record available at https://lccn.loc.gov/2023007107

Editor: Jennifer Lombardo
Copyeditor: Michele Suchomel-Casey
Designer: Deanna Paternostro

The photographs in this book are used by permission and through the courtesy of: Cover SALMONNEGRO-STOCK/Shutterstock.com; pp. 4, 8–9, 10, 12, 14, 16, 29 (left) Everett Collection/Shutterstock.com; p. 6 Yevgenij_D/Shutterstock.com; p. 18 M&N/Alamy Stock Photo; p. 19 APN Photography/Shutterstock.com; p. 22 Cesar Chavez visita a colegio Cesar Chavez/Wikimedia Commons; p. 24 Rena Schild/ Shutterstock.com; p. 25 Richard Thornton/Shutterstock.com; p. 27 Robert P. Alvarez/Shutterstock.com; p. 29 (right) Jana Shea/ Shutterstock.com.



CPSIA compliance information: Batch #CSCSQ24: For further information contact Cavendish Square Publishing LLC at 1-877-980-4450.

Printed in the United States of America

# CONTENTS

This painting from 1847 shows the Battle of Palo Alto, a battle of the Mexican-American War that took place on May 8, 1846.

# BECOMING AMERICAN BY FORCE

Chapter One

In 1845, the United States government decided to annex, or add to the country, what is now the state of Texas. However, Mexico still claimed this territory. The two countries then fought in what is now called the Mexican-American War. The United States won, Texas and other states were added to the country, and everyone living in those areas—who had previously been Mexican citizens—suddenly became Americans.

Even before the war, many U.S. citizens had treated Mexicans poorly. After the war, this treatment continued and was added to by the U.S. government. For many years, Mexican Americans didn't have the same rights other Americans had. In the 1960s and 1970s, the Mexican American civil rights movement—also known as the Chicano Movement—worked to overcome **stereotypes** and fight for the same treatment as all U.S. citizens.

**Fast Fact**

All or part of the states of California, New Mexico, Oklahoma, Kansas, Arizona, Utah, Nevada, Colorado, and Wyoming were once part of Mexico.

# WHAT DOES "CHICANO" MEAN?

In the 1940s, young people of Mexican descent who were born in the United States began calling themselves Chicano (for men) or Chicana (for women). It was a sign of their pride in their Mexican **culture** and heritage, or family history. In the 1960s, they gave their civil rights movement this name.

Not every Mexican American chooses to call themselves Chicano. Some prefer the term Latino, which refers to people from Latin America—countries where the official language is based in Latin, such as Spanish, French, or Portuguese. Others call themselves Hispanic, which refers to people who speak Spanish. It's polite to ask people what they call themselves instead of choosing a title for them.

Brazil's official language is Portuguese, so Brazilians are Latino, but not Hispanic. People from Suriname, whose official language is Dutch, and Guyana, whose official language is English, are neither.

**Fast Fact**

In 1854, the United States and Mexico finalized the Gadsden Purchase. The United States agreed to pay Mexico $10 million for lands that became part of Arizona and New Mexico.

## Broken Promises

The Treaty of Guadalupe Hidalgo officially marked the end of the Mexican-American War in 1848. It guaranteed constitutional rights to people living in the conquered lands. The treaty stated that Mexican people living in these lands must either move within Mexico's new borders or join the United States and abandon their Mexican loyalties.

However, the U.S. government broke some of its promises. For example, the treaty promised that Mexicans who owned land would be able to keep it. However, when white settlers started moving into the new American Southwest, they often took land by force—and white judges nearly always sided with the settlers if these claims were brought to court.

For years after the war, there was **racism** against Mexicans who decided to stay within the new U.S. borders, even though they were now U.S. citizens. Americans were traveling from the East Coast to settle in these new lands, and they began to outnumber people of Mexican descent. Many people in the United States believed in the idea of Manifest Destiny—the belief that God wanted the United States to stretch across North America. This belief also made many Americans feel that they had the right to take these western lands in any way they could.

Some Americans took the land by falsely reporting to the government that the Mexican Americans who owned the land

People traveled west in large groups called "wagon trains." They were given this name because of the covered wagons that were used to transport belongings.

## Fast Fact

Manifest Destiny was also very harmful to the Native Americans who already lived in the areas the United States wanted to claim. Many Native Americans were killed by white settlers who moved onto their land.

were being disloyal to the country. Some used the legal system to cheat the Mexican Americans, many of whom didn't speak English, out of their land. Others simply hurt or killed Mexican Americans and moved onto the land they had owned. These actions were called "land grabs."

The discovery of gold in California brought thousands of white miners to the new state.

# FACING DISCRIMINATION

Chapter Two

Land grabs increased when gold was found in California in the late 1840s. White settlers oppressed Mexican Americans in California and other areas in many ways, including by **lynching** them. Mob violence against innocent Mexican immigrants and Mexican Americans was common. Since law enforcement did not protect them, Mexicans created groups of "bandits" in an attempt to scare the white newcomers away and take back what was rightfully theirs.

## Looking for Work

In the late 1800s, railroads, farming, and mining were booming industries in the American West. More workers were needed. Mexicans traveled north of the border to find a growing number of jobs that paid higher wages than they could find in Mexico—although these wages were low for the work that was being done. White Americans felt Mexicans and Mexican Americans were taking jobs away from them,

**Fast Fact**

**Historians believe that between 1840 and 1930, at least 5,000 Mexicans and Mexican Americans were lynched. These lynchings mainly happened in Texas, California, Arizona, and New Mexico.**

**In the mid-1800s, the transcontinental railroad project employed many people. Although most of the workers were people of color, white people took credit for the finished product, shown here.**

even though they often didn't want to do any of the jobs available to people of Mexican descent.

The Mexican Revolution brought more Mexican immigrants to the United States in 1910. This led to more violence on the U.S.–Mexico border as the United States enforced tougher immigration laws.

Members of the Texas Rangers, a state law enforcement agency, committed some of the most violent attacks against

## FORCED DEPORTATION

During the Great Depression in the 1930s, anti-Mexican racism fed by unrealistic fears over job loss grew to a point where individuals and the government began deporting Mexicans and Mexican Americans, or kicking them out of the country. In some cases, employers drove their workers to the border and told them not to come back. In others, local governments **raided** houses, gathering places, and hospitals to take Mexicans and Mexican Americans to the border.

Overall, about 2 million people—more than half of whom were American citizens of Mexican descent—were deported during this time. Some left before they could be forced to. Unfair deportation still happens today.

### Fast Fact

Although the United States had strict, or tough, immigration laws, employers who wanted cheap labor would break those laws to bring Mexicans into the country.

Mexican Americans in the early 1900s. The rangers committed and allowed many shootings and hangings. By 1930, nearly 600 Mexican Americans in Texas had been killed, and thousands more had been driven off their land. Newspaper coverage contributed to greater fear and discrimination, or unfair treatment, against those of Mexican descent. After reading stories in the newspapers, which were written by white reporters, white

Americans believed it was Mexican Americans, rather than law enforcement, who were at fault for the violence. In fact, Mexican Americans in Texas weren't allowed to go out after dark.

## Separated in the Southwest

The increase in Mexican immigrants coming into the United States also led to **segregation** throughout the southwestern states. Even

**This sign from 1933 shows that Spanish-speaking workers and English-speaking workers were segregated into camps that were 1 mile (1.6 kilometers) apart.**

## Fast Fact

**A common stereotype against Mexicans and other people from foreign countries is that those who don't speak English aren't smart. This false belief was often used to justify taking advantage of Mexicans.**

though Mexican immigrants were playing an important role in the U.S. economy, many Americans didn't like that they were different. Many local businesses put up signs that said "No Mexicans Allowed" or "Whites Only."

Segregated schools became common in states such as California and Texas, where there were separate buildings called "Mexican schools." The government allowed this, saying that Mexican American children needed a special environment where they could be taught English. However, segregated schools had older books, fewer teachers, and some of the most rundown school buildings. Mexican American children received a much worse education than children at white-only schools.

Like the Black-only school shown here, Mexican-only schools were often overcrowded. Chicanos won a court case against segregated schools seven years before the landmark *Brown v. Board of Education* case.

# FIGHTING BACK

Chapter Three

Mexican Americans and other Latinos have fought for equal rights for decades. The early victories in the movement were mostly in the courts. For example, in 1947, the court case of *Mendez v. Westminster* ruled that segregated schools in Orange County, California, were against the 14th Amendment, or change, to the U.S. Constitution. This amendment grants equal protection under the law to all American citizens.

However, the official beginning of the Chicano Movement, also known as "El Movimiento" ("The Movement" in Spanish), came in the 1960s. Chicanos began to organize, and they gained greater power by helping John F. Kennedy become president. He was grateful for their votes, so he listened to the things the Chicano community wanted.

**Fast Fact**

In 1929, a group called the League of United Latin American Citizens (LULAC) was formed. Its purpose was to end discrimination and to promote education for Mexican Americans. Today, LULAC is the oldest Latino civil rights group in the United States.

## Getting Organized

In the early 1960s, Black Americans had already

gotten the country's attention with their own fight for equality. Chicanos realized they could create real change by organizing a huge group of people that would work together. Their focus

## Fast Fact

Before the movement, the term "Chicano" had often been used as a hurtful word to describe children of Mexican migrants. Younger Mexican American **activists** decided to use the name as a symbol of determination and pride in their Mexican roots.

**One of the goals of the Chicano Movement was greater political power for Latinos. This photo from 1970 shows Chicanos with posters supporting Jesse (Jess) Unruh for California governor.**

was on voting and political rights, educational equality, farm workers' rights, and land grants that were never honored by the U.S. government.

Every good organization needs leaders, and the Chicano Movement was no different. One of its most recognizable leaders was a man named Rodolfo "Corky" Gonzales. After a career as a boxer, he became interested in politics. During Kennedy's presidential campaign, Gonzales registered more

**One way Gonzales's important activist work was recognized in Denver, Colorado, was by naming a library after him.**

Cesar Chavez worked hard to help Chicano farm workers get better working conditions and legal protections.

Chapter Four

# THE FIGHT CONTINUES

Rodolfo Gonzales played a large leadership role in the cities, but other leaders arose among the farm workers in the countryside, especially Cesar Chavez and Dolores Huerta. In 1962, they founded the National Farm Workers Association (NFWA). This later became known as the United Farm Workers of America (UFWA).

In 1965, Chavez and Huerta organized a strike by California grape pickers and asked the nation to **boycott** grapes grown in California. They started gaining support from the public, which eventually led to other boycotts involving lettuce growers and wine makers. Their work paid off when the Agricultural Labor Relations Act was passed in 1975. This law gave the farm workers the right to collective bargaining, or working as a group to set up their conditions of employment.

### Fast Fact

**Undocumented** workers are an important part of the U.S. economy. They do many jobs other Americans don't want to do. Every year, they pay billions of dollars in taxes, but their lack of documentation means they often can't get the benefits their taxes pay for.

## Making Progress

The Chicano Movement was at its strongest during the 1960s

**In 2012, Dolores Huerta was awarded the Presidential Medal of Freedom for her activist work in the 1960s and 1970s.**

and early 1970s, but activists have still made progress in later years. For example, in 1986, the Immigration Reform and Control Act was passed. This act gave some undocumented workers the chance to obtain, or get, legal U.S. citizenship. Then, in 1989, Dr. Lauro Cavazos was appointed secretary of education. She became the first Latino to serve as part of a U.S. president's cabinet, or closest group of advisers.

# MARCHING FOR EQUALITY

In 1966, Chavez and Huerta organized a protest march. On March 17, about 100 farm workers set out from Delano, California, near the U.S.–Mexico border. About one month later, they arrived in California's capital, Sacramento. On the 280-mile (450 kilometers) journey, hundreds of supporters joined them.

This march made the U.S. government as well as private employers take notice of Chicanos and their demands. While it didn't completely get rid of discrimination against farm workers, it won the NFWA some huge victories, including its first **union** contract.

This picture shows a man who participated in the 1966 march to Sacramento holding a photo of the march.

In 1994, Proposition 187, which denied many forms of public assistance to undocumented immigrants, was passed in California. This was met with massive protests, so Proposition 187 was overturned in 1997.

**Fast Fact**

A group of Chicanos called the Brown Berets, modeled after the Black Panthers, believed in arming themselves for protection. Their protests focused mainly on the issues of violence and racism against Chicanos.

In 2006, Mexican American activists set up demonstrations across the country in response to proposals in Congress that would make undocumented immigrants criminals. These were the largest demonstrations of this kind in the United States since the height of the Chicano Movement. Between March and May of that year, almost 1 million protesters marched against the proposals. Many of the organizers and participants were high school and college students. Spanish-speaking newspapers and television stations helped get the message out about the protests.

## More to Do

Although the Chicano Movement won many victories, Mexican Americans—and all Latinos in the United States—still face a lot of discrimination. Racism and violence against Mexicans and other Latinos skyrocketed after Donald Trump was elected president in 2016. During his campaign, he made many false statements about Mexican immigrants and promised to build a wall on the southern border to keep them out. His words created a lot of fear, which led to discrimination against Latinos.

**In 2019, many Americans found out that the U.S. government was separating immigrant families who were seeking asylum, or safety from violence in their home country. Protests such as the one shown here were common during this time.**

Today, Latinos and their allies, or supporters, are still working on some of the main issues that were at least partially addressed during the Chicano Movement. For example, in 2013 and 2021, key protections in the Voting Rights Act of 1965 were taken away, again making it hard for many people of color to vote. Mexican Americans and other Latinos today are still fighting for their rights and an end to discrimination, continuing the work begun many years ago.

# PEOPLE TO KNOW

## Cesar Chavez

Chavez was born in Arizona on March 21, 1927. He and his family moved to California to become farm workers during the Great Depression. The treatment they received inspired him to work toward better conditions for farm workers.

## Gloria Anzaldua

Anzaldua was born on September 26, 1942. She was an activist and a poet who wrote about her experiences as both a Chicana and a member of the **LGBTQ+ community**. Her work inspired other LGBTQ+ Chicanas.

## Dolores Huerta

Huerta was born on April 10, 1930. She was a teacher in the 1950s in a California farming community. She saw so many mistreated and hungry students that she decided to become an activist to make life better for farm workers and their families.

## Rodolfo "Corky" Gonzales

Gonzales was born on June 18, 1928. He got his nickname from his uncle, who said that he was "always popping off like a cork" because of his strong opinions and fiery temper. He was an important leader of the Chicano Movement, especially in Denver, Colorado.

## Francisca Flores

Flores was born in San Diego, California, in 1913. As a young adult, she helped found a feminist organization where Chicanas, who were often ignored by men, could talk about politics. When she was in the hospital at age 26, Flores organized a strike for the nurses that helped them get a pay raise.

# THINK ABOUT IT!

1. What could the United States have done to help Mexicans after the Mexican-American War?
2. Why do you think it was important to Chicanos to gain more political power?
3. Why do you think the Chicano Movement is less well-known than the Black civil rights movement that happened at the same time?
4. What are some ways you can help Latinos gain equality and respect today?

# INDEX